Stages of Implementation

A GUIDE FOR YOUR JOURNEY TO KNOWLEDGE MANAGEMENT BEST PRACTICES

Carla O'Dell, Ph.D.

with

Farida Hasanali

Cindy Hubert

Kimberly Lopez

Peggy Odem

Cynthia Raybourn

AMERICAN PRODUCTIVITY
& QUALITY CENTER

American Productivity & Quality Center
123 North Post Oak Lane, Third Floor
Houston, TX 77024

Edited by Craig Henderson
Designed by Connie Choate

Manufactured in the United States of America

ISBN 1-928593-40-2

American Productivity & Quality Center
Web site address: www.apqc.org

Contents

Acknowledgments iv

Preface v

Introduction 1

Quiz: Where Are You Now? 9

Landmark 1: Getting Started 13

Landmark 2: Explore and Experiment 21

Landmark 3: Pilots and Knowledge
    Management Initiatives 27

Landmark 4: Expand and Support 35

Landmark 5: Institutionalize Knowledge Management 45

Packing List 57

About the Authors 59

About APQC 65

Acknowledgments

The American Productivity & Quality Center (APQC) would like to thank all of the organizations we have worked with to uncover the trends and best practices in the growing world of knowledge management (KM). Without the companies that sponsor our research—and especially those that are willing to impart their knowledge, experiences, and insights—we would not be able to share this valuable information with the public.

We extend a special thank-you to those organizations that sponsored our 1999–2000 consortium benchmarking effort, Successfully Implementing Knowledge Management, as well as those that participated as partner organizations and allowed our study team to examine and learn from their knowledge management practices. A significant amount of information in this book was gained during the Successfully Implementing Knowledge Management consortium learning forum.

Preface

Ever since the American Productivity & Quality Center formed in 1977, our goal has been to disseminate knowledge to help organizations perform more effectively. We've done that in numerous ways over the years, from developing improvement and measurement approaches to offering benchmarking studies, conferences, training courses, research services, and a variety of publications.

Our members and other customers have told us there is an emerging need for easy-to-use resource guides to help them communicate, understand, and implement programs and processes in a variety of functional areas. As a result, we've drawn on our experience and knowledge to produce APQC's Passport to Success book series.

We chose the title Passport to Success because these books are intended to guide you on what can be a difficult journey through somewhat foreign territory. Each book in this series provides readers with the mechanisms to gauge their current status, understand the components (or landmarks) of a successful initiative in a specific topic area, and determine how to proceed within their own organization.

These books also supplement the other "hands-on" support services and products APQC offers, so that we may provide you with integrated process improvement tools. To learn what else APQC provides in your area of interest, please visit our Web site at www.apqc.org or call 800-776-9676 (713-681-4020 outside the United States).

Introduction

The age of knowledge management "early adopters" is over. Hundreds of organizations, large and small, want to capitalize on what they know. They want to create, identify, capture, transfer, and reuse their valuable knowledge—in other words, "manage" it.

Knowledge management has evolved into a systematic process to:
- identify important knowledge,
- create a space and system for people to share what they know and create new knowledge,
- capture best practices and useful information in a form that other people can use in the future, and
- transfer that information and knowledge to others who can use it.

KM is not about just sharing documents. Knowledge includes what people know about how to make things work better, best practices, and lessons learned about any process—knowledge as "information in use." Of course, knowledge can't exist without information as well as experience. With good information, people can make better decisions and take intelligent action.

In conducting five years of knowledge management research and six KM consortium studies, the American Productivity & Quality

In January 2000, the *Guardian,* a British newspaper, announced that Prime Minister Tony Blair's government is proposing an electronic "knowledge network" for Whitehall. At the click of a mouse, ministers can get the "best three arguments" or "best five facts" in support of any of Blair's policies.

Center has studied and worked with dozens of organizations as they designed and implemented their KM initiatives. We recently revisited many of these organizations, searching for those that could serve as role models for successfully implementing KM. Our criteria included consideration of how well the organization had:

- created a business case and rationale for KM,
- tied KM to its mission,
- deployed a strategy for launching and expanding KM,
- achieved successful results, and
- developed an approach to understanding and measuring the impact of KM.

Among these best-practice organizations are Buckman Laboratories, Chevron Corporation, Hewlett-Packard Consulting, IBM Consulting Services, Nortel Networks, Schlumberger, Siemens AG, Shell Services, World Bank, and Xerox Corporation.

We studied in detail nine of the organizations that met our criteria, and their experiences form the basis of a significant discovery. In looking across the organizations, we were able to identify five stages common to successful KM implementation:

Stage 1: Getting Started

Stage 2: Explore and Experiment

Stage 3: Pilots and KM Initiatives

Stage 4: Expand and Support

Stage 5: Institutionalize KM

We draw on these early adopters and best-practice organizations to understand the critical success factors, options, and steps involved in implementing a successful KM initiative.

This book, which examines APQC's Road Map to Knowledge Management Results: Stages of Implementation™, enables readers to:

- understand their organization's position in the KM journey,
- see how others have successfully faced similar challenges,
- share techniques and "what works" at each stage, and
- know what might be done to move on.

Understanding the issues, seeing the signposts of problems and opportunities, and knowing the tools and tactics employed by others can help at any stage. Learning from experienced KM practitioners will provide you the opportunity to make new mistakes, not repeat those made by others in the past. By understanding the process and stages, readers will be better equipped to manage the process in their own organizations.

Each stage illustrated in Figure 1 (page 4) will be described as if it were distinct from the others. In reality, the stages flow into each other, as different parts of the organization move at different speeds and various elements fall into place. For example, not all organizations begin their journey with Stage 1. Sometimes Stage 2 marks the beginning of the KM journey because a manager simply wants to share knowledge in his or her business unit and sees KM as the solution to a problem. At the World Bank and Xerox, these grassroots efforts provided compelling stories when management began to explore whether KM would work for them. The early advocates were quick to point out the success, learn from it, and capitalize on it to build energy for expansion.

Some firms move through the stages very quickly, learning from early adopters and barely stopping to notice they have moved to a whole new level of implementation. As we begin to describe the stages in detail, it is important to remember that the stages are a composite of the experiences of many companies.

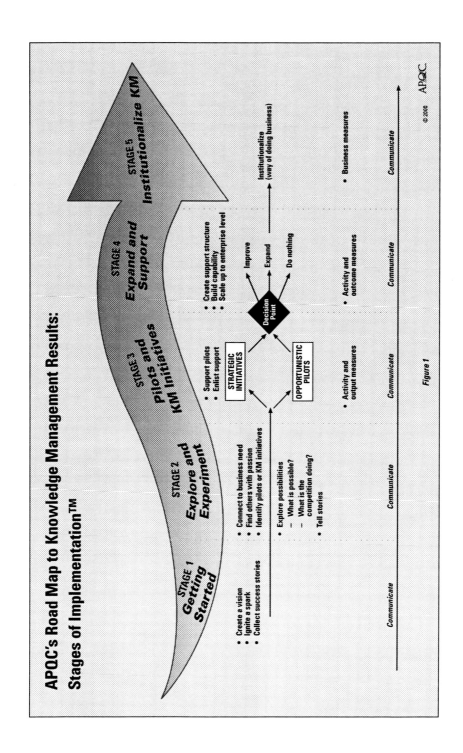

APQC's Road Map to Knowledge Management Results:
Stages of Implementation™

STAGE 1 Getting Started
- Create a vision
- Ignite a spark
- Collect success stories

Communicate

STAGE 2 Explore and Experiment
- Connect to business need
- Find others with passion
- Identify pilots or KM initiatives

- Explore possibilities
  — What is possible?
  — What is the competition doing?
- Tell stories

- Activity and output measures

Communicate

STAGE 3 Pilots and KM Initiatives
- Support pilots
- Enlist support

STRATEGIC INITIATIVES

Decision Point

OPPORTUNISTIC PILOTS

- Activity and output measures

Communicate

STAGE 4 Expand and Support
- Create support structure
- Build capability
- Scale up to enterprise level

Improve
Expand
Do nothing

- Activity and outcome measures

Communicate

STAGE 5 Institutionalize KM

Institutionalize (way of doing business)

- Business measures

Communicate

APQC
© 2000

Figure 1

The reader will notice themes that transcend the stages but change in appearance as the KM effort evolves. Some of these themes are:

- creating a knowledge-sharing culture,
- gaining buy-in,
- measuring, and
- creating a business case for knowledge management.

Culture and buy-in will be addressed in the landmark chapters, which highlight each stage of KM implementation. The issue of the business case for KM illustrates how these issues change over time. It is a pitfall of new KM initiatives to try to address the business case (or measurement) prematurely. Measurement needs tend to reflect both the stage and the business case.

THE BUSINESS CASE AND MEASURES FOR KM

Both the business case and measurement standards vary dramatically by stage. A formal business case, with financial return on investment (ROI), is neither possible nor necessary during Stage 1. At this stage, champions have a belief in the value of knowledge to enhance the organization's effectiveness, and they can express that relationship. There also may be a desire to leverage new connectivity tools.

The KM business cases in Stages 1 and 2 tend to be "if ... then" statements related to specific needs. For example: "If we can get the right information earlier in the new product development process, then we can invest heavily in some projects and kill others more quickly. This will save money and increase returns." "If I share and use knowledge, then I can make partner sooner."

Stage 1, Getting Started, tends to be funded through "sweat equity": the time champions spend squeezing in the KM effort with the support of a sympathetic boss. Formal funding issues do not arise until Stage 2, and even then most of the cost is contributed time.

DEBBIE
NITIN
LIZ
MARGE
MEG
LALITA
BRUCE

By Stage 2, Explore and Experiment, the business case for proceeding is based on the soundness of the pilot strategy, the urgency of the problems being addressed, and the promise of gains from the pilots.

By Stage 3, Pilots and KM Initiatives, the leadership wants to see a measurable gain and ROI from the selected pilots. The formal need for a budget arises in this stage, when the specific spending rationale for labor and time needs to be made. At this stage, the leadership also wants to see plans and measures for return on investment in the pilots. Equally important to the champions is learning how to make KM effective.

At Stage 4, Expand and Support, the questions about where the accountability will reside in the organization structure are intricately bound with the spending issues. Typically, authorization comes from the top. Once KM becomes part of the organization's operational model and structure, the KM function has to annually justify the need for central infrastructure to maintain the competency. KM is now exposed to the same internal budget debates as any other major expenditure.

Once the strategic decision is made to make KM a management competency (usually at Stage 4), it becomes important to implement it cost effectively, not to ask whether to implement it at all. As the effort matures, difficult questions about costs are asked, but "Is knowledge capture, transfer, and use a good thing to support?" is not one of them. We have seen the same phenomenon in earlier eras with total quality management, process improvement, and team-based approaches. Now, diving into e-commerce and Web-based marketing, the business model precedes the proof.

By Stage 5, Institutionalize KM, funds to sustain and expand knowledge management know-how are needed. There must be clear indicators that KM has resulted in positive effects, which are rarely in isolation from other interventions. The objectives of Stage 5 are to build widespread competency in KM and sharing, integrate KM into the management model of the organization, and spread that competency across the organization. By this stage, KM is recognized as adding value to the organization. It is important to measure that value, sustain it, and cultivate it over time.

In every successful large-scale KM initiative we have examined, an important senior champion or group saw the strategic value and endorsed what became a significant investment. This person initially made a calculated leap of faith based on a compelling business rationale or vision, not purely a return on investment calculation. This does not mean that measures and ROI aren't important; they are. But alone they are not enough to cause KM to be institutionalized as a way of working.

Figure 2, page 8, shows the dominant business rationale for KM in some of the Stage 4 and Stage 5 organizations we have studied recently.

Measurement is a more difficult matter. However, one would be hard-pressed to find an organization satisfied with how it measures the impact of KM or an organization that has a complete, systematic approach to measuring it. None of our early adopters have found the

EXPERT ADVICE

- Develop a clear picture of how KM will support the business model. This is essential at every stage. Over time, the model will become clearer, more tangible, and more compelling as the organization gains experience with KM.

- Develop measures—anecdotal and quantitative—to provide guidance for understanding the impact of KM on the business model. Use measures as guideposts.

- Broadly communicate the results of the pilots, both the business results and the process lessons.

- Embed the costs in other activities to which the organization has already committed resources.

FIGURE 2: The Business Rationale Behind the Business Case

	Chevron	HP Consulting	Siemens AG	World Bank	Xerox	IBM Global Services	Buckman Laboratories
Cost Reduction	++		++				
Reuse of Knowledge and Lessons Learned	++	++		++	++	++	++
Speed		++				++	++
Innovation		++				++	
Reuse of KM Know-how			++	++	++		
Rebranding and Differentiation				++	++		
Improved Quality of Knowledge		++		++		++	++

magic bullet that satisfies all of the requirements of a complete measurement system. Rather, the organizations approach measurement in different ways and with differing degrees of quantitative precision, depending upon stage of evolution, direction of KM activities, and varying degrees of need to prove value.

In the earliest stages, formal measurement is rarely required or used. As KM becomes more structured and widespread, the need for measurement steadily increases. As KM becomes institutionalized— a way of doing business—the importance of KM-specific measures diminishes and the need to measure the effectiveness of knowledge-intensive business processes replaces them. Eventually, organizational performance measures such as cycle time to develop new products, time to train new employees, and sales of complex products should reflect the value of KM without necessarily being able to ferret out the KM contribution. Throughout the stages, we will point to some of the stage-appropriate measurement approaches used by leading organizations.

Where Are You Now?

The following quiz is designed to help you determine the current status of your organization in terms of APQC's Road Map to Knowledge Management Results. If you agree with the majority of statements within each of the following groupings, your organization likely resides in, or possibly has passed through, that particular stage of knowledge management implementation. By identifying the point at which you're starting, you will be better suited to navigate toward points beyond the horizon.

Stage 1
- Knowledge management has emerged as a topic of interest in our organization.
- At least a few employees have explored the benefits of KM for our organization.
- Someone in our organization has had a personal stake in developing interest and action in KM.
- We have learned about KM through participation in consortia or conferences.
- We have created a high-level rationale or vision for why our organization should pursue KM.

Stage 2
- We have a cross-functional KM exploratory group, such as a "working group" or steering committee.
- We have enlisted an executive sponsor willing to support the exploration of KM.
- We have identified some successful, internal grassroots efforts already under way in KM.
- Our IT organization is interested in actively supporting KM initiatives.
- We have collected stories of how knowledge sharing has helped our organization in the past.
- We have identified pilots, allowing us to demonstrate how KM could benefit our organization.
- We have secured ownership and buy-in from those pilot areas.
- We have secured funding for the pilots.

Stage 3
- We have designed pilot approaches and have implementation strategies in place.
- We have launched KM pilots such as communities of practice or an interactive KM intranet.
- We have enlisted and trained facilitators and leaders for these pilots.
- We have pilot measures and indicators in place, as well as a system for tracking and reporting them.
- We have created strategies for learning from our KM initiatives.
- We have mapped strategies for expanding these pilot initiatives across the organization.

Stage 4

- The results of the pilots have raised demand for KM in other units or processes.
- We have begun to market the KM strategy throughout the organization.
- We have deployed KM at an enterprisewide level.
- We have an expansion or replication strategy in place for our KM initiative.
- We have identified the resources required to expand our KM efforts.

Stage 5

- KM is linked directly to the success of our business model.
- Our KM initiatives are widely deployed throughout the organization.
- All managers and employees are trained to use KM-enabling technologies.
- We methodically assess our KM strategy, identify gaps, and outline processes to close the gaps.
- We have a formal support structure in place to maintain KM.
- Rewards and recognition programs are aligned with KM in our organization.
- Sharing knowledge has become the norm at our organization.

Getting Started

The fire to manage knowledge starts with the spark of inspiration. Someone becomes inspired with the vision of what it would be like if the organization could effectively support human knowledge capture, transfer, and use (a.k.a. knowledge management).

Energized by his or her vision, this champion (also characterized as an advocate or "evangelist") begins to search for opportunities to share the vision with others and demonstrate the value of KM to the organization. For early adopters of KM, this stage was perhaps the most difficult. Now that more is known about KM, this stage proceeds more easily and quickly.

The champion at this first stage of implementation has four key tasks:

1. Make the concepts of KM real.
2. Identify others to join the cause.
3. Look for windows of opportunity.
4. Capitalize on the Internet, and enlist the IT department to provide tools and a balanced view of KM.

MAKE THE CONCEPTS OF KM REAL

There are four ways to make the concepts of KM real to early listeners in your organization: defining it, storytelling, connecting with other initiatives, and benchmarking.

Defining KM

The central task for the KM advocate at this stage is to create a vision that inspires others to explore of how managing knowledge might contribute value to the enterprise and its people. The challenge is to create a tangible picture and clear understanding of what KM means to the organization while connecting, at a personal level, with real problems, opportunities, and values. At this early stage, simple definitions, told in lay language, work best. APQC's definition of knowledge management should be modified to fit your situation.

APQC's Definition of Knowledge Management

Knowledge management is the systematic process of identifying, capturing, and transferring information and knowledge people can use to improve.

For example, senior leaders at Hewlett-Packard Consulting created a vision for the entire HP Consulting knowledge management initiative that helped define what knowledge management meant for them: "Our consultants feel and act as if they have the knowledge of the entire organization at their fingertips when they consult with customers. They know exactly where to go to find information. They are eager to share knowledge as well as leverage others' experience in order to deliver more value to customers. We will recognize those consultants that share and those that leverage others' knowledge and experience as the most valuable members of the HP team."

Chevron not only defines the term but also identifies the people involved, states behavioral expectations, and addresses the "whys" of knowledge management. The company defines knowledge management as processes, tools, and behaviors that deliver the right content to the right people at the right time and in the right context so that they can make the best decisions, exploit business opportunities, and innovate.

Siemens used author Peter Senge's definition: Knowledge is the capacity for effective action. The company added that "knowledge management refers to all systematic activities for creation and sharing of knowledge so that knowledge can be used for the success of the organization."

Storytelling

Storytelling has become a valuable tool for engaging the imagination of people in organizations about how managing knowledge might work for them. At the World Bank, the term knowledge management risked being confused with some kind of computer system—a "brain in the sky" that was unrealistic and irrelevant to the goals of the organization. Storytelling proved to be the most attention-getting and memorable way to build understanding and interest. It enabled managers and staff members to understand the concept and, by analogy, reinvent the concept for their own work environments.

They began with stories about a staff person in an underdeveloped country who needed the best information on treating malaria in a particular situation. They connected with others who had experience and rapidly received answers that could help. Listeners could identify with the story, prompting them to imagine what else they might be able to do if only they could connect with others.

Sometimes painful reminders of the cost of not knowing (CONK) are more powerful than stories of gains. At Xerox, not knowing that a technician had fixed a $40,000 machine with a 50 cent part could have cost the company plenty. Fortunately, because of the Eureka knowledge-sharing system, a technician in Brazil did know of the fellow technician's feat, and other machines were fixed rather than returned at a significant loss to Xerox.

Connecting With Other Initiatives

One successful approach is to link KM to other well-known initiatives and values, such as "The Learning Organization." This was an important tactic at Chevron, which had a commitment to and history of systematic quality management.

Benchmarking

Benchmarking is important at this stage because it can provide a compelling reason to change. For example, data about the productivity and cost levels of competitors was a powerful motivator for

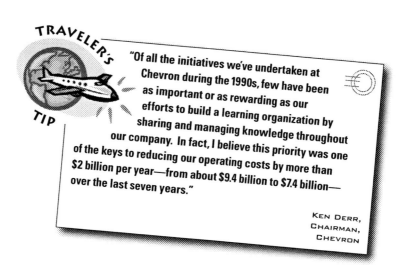

TRAVELER'S TIP

"Of all the initiatives we've undertaken at Chevron during the 1990s, few have been as important or as rewarding as our efforts to build a learning organization by sharing and managing knowledge throughout our company. In fact, I believe this priority was one of the keys to reducing our operating costs by more than $2 billion per year—from about $9.4 billion to $7.4 billion— over the last seven years."

KEN DERR,
CHAIRMAN,
CHEVRON

Chevron to look at innovative ways to catch up. HP Consulting was motivated by knowing that other consulting firms were competing on knowledge. Every APQC partner has used benchmarking of other firms' KM practices to help them at this stage.

Other actions a champion can take at this stage to connect people with the value of KM at a personal level are:

- provide KM articles to read,
- take people to KM conferences so they can see what others have done,
- provide benchmarking data, and
- take part in a consortium benchmarking effort to see firsthand what others have done and accomplished with KM.

Although the last tactic may sound self-serving, APQC has found that a large number of organizations that have successfully implemented KM, as well as those in the early stages of implementation, believe they have advanced more rapidly as a result of their participation in an APQC consortium learning forum.

IDENTIFY OTHERS TO JOIN THE CAUSE

The second task is for the champion to find others who might be doing something that "looks like KM." The KM champion and other advocates need to be great boundary-spanners because potential allies likely reside in other silos in the organization.

Successful advocates find others by asking themselves some of the following questions:

- Are there existing knowledge-sharing groups with which I can connect?
- What are we already doing that might be related to KM?
- What is the personal value of sharing knowledge that people find inspiring?

LOOK FOR WINDOWS OF OPPORTUNITY

Any good change agent looks for the biggest pain, gain, or opportunity to show the value and relevance of KM to the organization. At Chevron, it was the need for dramatic cost-cutting that energized the quality organization (the early champions of KM) to use benchmarking and best-practice sharing. In the World Bank, it was the vision of the new president, Jim Wolfensohn, and pressure from other competitive lenders.

Fortunately for Xerox, the organization's five-year plan was under development just as KM appeared on the horizon. In 1995 Dan Holtshouse, director of corporate strategy and knowledge initiatives, was part of an effort to transition Xerox to "The Document Company." Astonished at the large turnout for an APQC/Arthur Andersen conference on knowledge management in 1995, he came away believing that KM would be important to Xerox customers and that the time was right for Xerox to build competency in it.

Convinced it had potential, Chairman Paul Allaire asked Holtshouse's team to explore the role of KM in the next five-year plan for Xerox. In effect, Xerox went seamlessly through Stage 1 to Stage 2.

ROADBLOCKS TO SUCCESS

- Ignoring your own corporate culture/history to avoid pitfalls and baggage that might be associated with knowledge management
- Attempting to sell an enterprisewide approach without building evidence first
- Asking for a large budget before creating a compelling value proposition

---

How to Find Windows of Opportunity

- Interview people involved in strategic initiatives to see if knowledge-sharing principles can help.
- Talk to internal consulting groups.
- Use your own relationships to find opportunities.

CAPITALIZE ON THE INTERNET, AND ENLIST THE IT DEPARTMENT

Information technology (IT) is a powerful and necessary enabler for KM. The new generation of IT leaders has the opportunity to stand out as strategic business visionaries, not just "techies," by advocating a balanced and integrated social and technical solution.

IT functionality per se may not be critical at this stage, but the IT organization is often a catalyst to use emerging Internet technologies to support KM efforts. For example, when Chevron reorganized, the IT organization stepped up to meet the need for a central group to support the KM effort. In fact, Chevron's IT organization serves as a role model for next-generation communities of practice (CoPs). The company spent more than $200 million establishing a common IT platform so all Chevron associates could communicate and share. This newfound capability made deeper and broader participation in KM possible.

Knowledge management has benefited enormously from the huge investments in information technology in recent years. In the late 1990s, IT investment was increasing at the blistering rate of 15 percent per year in the United States, with actual capacity increasing twice as fast because of a dramatic decline in prices. With the IT investment has come a blossoming of KM tools that address some of the most nagging problems that have plagued KM implementation in the past. Once Bill Gates and Microsoft threw their weight behind knowledge management *(Business @ the Speed of Thought,* 1999), KM entered the IT mainstream.

APQC found the following developments in the best-practice organizations we've studied:

1. IT for knowledge management has become affordable for most organizations.
2. "Smarter" search engines have enabled information to be organized from a sociocultural and user perspective rather than codified according to a library system.
3. The rise of the knowledge portal has contributed to the "branding" of knowledge management in organizations.
4. IT tools for knowledge management are more complicated than they appear, and they require significant energy to implement and sustain.
5. IT is helping to build KM into work processes, from project management to product development to selling.
6. The importance of making connections—of people to people and of people to information—is the driver to use IT in KM initiatives.

Expert Advice

- Benchmarking and success stories create a compelling picture of what is possible.
- A single champion/advocate must find cohorts, preferably ones with clout in the organization, quickly.

Explore and Experiment

S tage 2 is the turning point from individual interest or local efforts in knowledge management to an organizational experiment. It is characterized both by the decision to explore "how KM might work here" and an evolution from individual passion to organizational action. By this time the original champions have successfully connected to a need and a senior executive sponsor.

The central task at this stage is to formulate the first iteration of the KM strategy, determine how it fits with the business, identify pilots to test the concept, and deploy the initial steps for moving forward. A small group usually is ordained to undertake this work on behalf of the organization.

KEY ACTIVITIES FOR STAGE 2
1. Form a cross-functional KM task force.
2. Select pilots or identify current local efforts.
3. Find resources to support the pilots.

FORM A CROSS-FUNCTIONAL KM TASK FORCE

There usually is an obvious core group to serve on the task force. This group often is made up of advocates enlisted in Stage 1 and other cross-functional representatives. At Siemens, for example, there were already several KM initiatives under way in numerous business units. Key participants in these initiatives became the nucleus of a KM community of practice to capture lessons, encourage learning, and promote common methodologies across all the initiatives.

After forming the task force, it is necessary to enlist this cross-functional group to find pilots or opportunities that will be used to test and understand how KM practices and principles can be applied in a selected focus area. All of the advanced KM organizations APQC has studied—those successfully implementing KM—relied heavily on benchmarking with other firms at this stage to learn how they had developed a strategy and then piloted and managed their KM efforts.

We asked several successful knowledge management implementers which functions were heavily involved in the design of their KM initiatives. The breadth of cross-functional involvement is illustrated in Figure 3.

SELECT PILOTS OR IDENTIFY CURRENT LOCAL EFFORTS

The selection or identification of KM pilots is the central goal of Stage 2. We have seen two types of pilots: strategic and opportunistic.

Strategic pilots can take the form of creating an intranet-driven infrastructure, entering a new market, or developing a new product. They are more visible and involve higher risk, but the payoffs are enormous if they work.

The knowledge management team at HP Consulting began by launching a pilot with a strategic business unit, the HPC SAP practice in North America. The leader of this practice felt it was essential for the few knowledgeable consultants in the western United States to share with all SAP consultants in North America the knowledge and skills gained from the new "Rapid SAP" process.

FIGURE 3: Groups Involved in Design of KM Initiatives					
Chevron Corporation	HP Consulting	Siemens ICN	Siemens AG	World Bank Group	Xerox
• Quality • HR • CITC (Corporate Information Technology Co.) • Operating Companies • Marketing and Sales • Technical Library	• VP/GM • HPC Leadership Team • SAP Practice Leader • KM Consulting Team • IT Staff • HP Consultants	• Executive Team • Communication Service • IT • Information Services/ Library • Intranet • Web team • Marketing and Sales • All Levels of Management	• CKM and Council • KM Developers and Consultants • CoP KM • ICN ShareNet Managers • Corporate Procurement and Logistics	• Executive Strategy Group • Operations (Sector Boards) • Information Services Library • IT • Intranet/ Web Team • KM Leaders	• Corporate • KM Task Force • Strategy • Quality • Business Intelligence • HR *Eureka:* • *Xerox* PARC • World-wide Customer Service

The team had already made efforts to capture related documents and information; it made the information available through a database. Unfortunately, the database was not heavily used, and there were no processes to keep the material up to date. The practice leader could not understand why the SAP consultants were not using the database and why it was so hard to get people to share and leverage this knowledge. The KM team used this leader's frustration and commitment as a springboard to launch Project OWL (Orchestrating Wisdom and Learning).

With opportunistic pilots, the tactic can be either to uncover grassroots efforts and learn from them or to select local, smaller-scale pilots.

The World Bank, for example, discovered KM activities under way in Africa, the Education Group, and other areas. These efforts provided strong evidence that knowledge was flowing freely and activities were abundant in areas where communities of interest existed. Where there were no communities, there was little activity. Based on the World Bank's experience, the KM team learned that neither connecting nor collecting could be effectively conducted unless CoPs (thematic groups, as they are now called) were in place. These grassroots efforts help shape the strategy.

Xerox's Eureka community began as a field experiment by Xerox PARC (Palo Alto Research Center) in the French Customer Service organization. Eureka is the name given the database used by the community of field technicians to share validated tips and knowledge. The initiative proved to be a huge test bed for the entire sequence of enlisting, validating, and sharing field knowledge. Several years of experience with Eureka and a strong champion provided powerful evidence of the sociotechnical nature of KM.

Expert Advice: Criteria for Selecting Pilot Groups

- The pilot issue is important to the business.
- Success will lead to demonstrable results.
- There is a champion/sponsor with resources.
- The pilot group is willing to share what it has learned.
- Lessons are transferable to other situations or units; they are not unique to those units.

FIND RESOURCES TO SUPPORT THE PILOTS

At this stage, the KM group charged with supporting the pilots must find the resources to do so. The primary resources that are necessary are skilled staff members to facilitate the pilots and help employees discover a new way of working. Able facilitators usually are already in the organization, often on the KM team. They need authorization from management to redirect their time to support the initiative. Additionally, information technology applications often need to be created or modified at this stage.

A large organization may go through each stage of knowledge management implementation at various times. For example, one KM initiative may be ready to move into Stage 3 whereas initiatives in other areas are just being defined and therefore may still be in Stage 1 or Stage 2. Stage 2 ends with the kickoff of one or more pilots.

Pilots and Knowledge Management Initiatives

The goals of Stage 3 are to conduct successful pilots, provide evidence of KM's business value, and capture lessons learned. The process of conducting pilots—and describing their forms—is so detailed that it is reserved for other writings.[1] For the KM practitioners responsible for the implementation of pilots, the following activities are critical.

KEY ACTIVITIES IN STAGE 3
1. Fund the pilots.
2. Develop KM approaches and methods that can be replicated and scaled up.
3. Capture lessons learned.

FUND THE PILOTS
Unless proposal of the pilots happens to luckily hit the right time in the budget cycle to be funded, the champion or KM practitioners

---

[1] *Other APQC publications provide detailed descriptions of advanced KM organizations' specific pilots and what they learned about implementing communities of practice, lessons-learned approaches, and vibrant best-practice repositories. (See the Packing List on page 57 of this book for suggestions.)*

will have to reallocate time and resources to the efforts. Every best-practice partner reported that a KM task force or oversight group existed to help free up these resources. This could be a steering committee, a cross-unit task force, or some existing body that provided overall supervision and support, including money and time. The following are a few examples:

- At the World Bank, funding came from a central resource as well from the pilot units in the form of time, people, and money donations. Not surprisingly, an increase in budget led to an increase in CoP formation.

- For Chevron, the corporate imperative for cost reduction allowed the consultants in the corporate quality organization to redirect their efforts to best-practice transfer, in conjunction with their other process improvement activities.

- HP Consulting's core KM team was already in place and had authorization from a senior partner to support the SAP pilot and learning communities.

- In the case of Xerox, resources for Eureka were provided by Xerox PARC, the Xerox France Customer Service organization, and later, Xerox Canada.

- At Siemens, the two units most active in knowledge management, the ICN division and Corporate Purchasing and Logistics, provided funding and support, with central support from the KM CoP as needed.

Start-up and implementation costs vary widely. Fifty-six percent of the advanced KM companies APQC has studied have spent more than $1 million on costs associated with Stages 1 through 3, whereas about half of the organizations in Stages 1 and 2 have spent less than $100,000. Annual maintenance requires at least the same level of investment. Leaders in firms at all stages are of the opinion that their KM budgets will increase in the future.

Money is one hurdle; the other is to find or create a group of experienced KM practitioners and free up enough of their time to support a pilot initiative. The people supporting pilots need key skills as well as knowledge of change management, project management, communication, and information technology for best-practice repositories and Web sites. The early champions and core KM team are the "rootstock" from which this group is started and grown.

DEVELOP KM APPROACHES AND METHODS THAT CAN BE REPLICATED AND SCALED UP

In the early stages of knowledge management, a common mistake is to build knowledge collections based on existing materials and without an active community of practitioners contributing to the effort. Total supply-driven efforts were rarely successful in the World Bank or any other organization APQC has studied. The efforts require tremendous resources, especially to create the supply, and they are rarely successful alone in getting people to refresh or use the resources. A more successful approach is to form communities by combining knowledge providers and knowledge users in a single, seamless community of practitioners.

The World Bank learned that the most successful KM results came from areas where the focus was on building active communities of experts. As a result, the pilot focus turned toward learning what made communities thrive.

The HP Consulting KM team focused on developing key knowledge processes and methodologies important to the consulting community and its work: Learning Communities (communities of practice), Knowledge Maps (analysis of knowledge gaps in a process, product, or solution), and Project Snapshots (the processes by which approaches, insights, and deliverables are captured from the experience of a project team).

At Xerox, Eureka went through multiple refinements. As the Xerox team learned how to identify experts to serve as validators, it also determined how to encourage and reward technicians for sharing and using their repair experiences and "fixes." Additionally, the team also ensured that the information technology would be approachable and rewarding to use.

Siemens used the experiences of its KM practitioners to build up a body of knowledge, methods, and templates that could be reused in other locations. This became the core intellectual capital of the KM CoP.

A KM Approach: Communities of Practice

Communities of practice are emerging as a new organizational form for creating knowledge-sharing relationships, promoting organizational learning, and implementing change. In a recent APQC study, 60 percent of the leading organizations practicing KM cited communities of practice as central to their knowledge management approaches (second only to intranet support).

Communities of practice have emerged as an effective way of creating, sharing, validating, and transferring tacit knowledge. Variously called communities of interest, communities of practice, learning communities, thematic groups, or knowledge networks, all best-practice organizations are using CoPs.

There are two emerging models for CoPs: informal and formal. The best-practice organizations APQC has examined have made

"Not so long ago, companies were reinvented by teams. Communities of practice may reinvent them yet again—if managers learn to cultivate these fertile organizational forms without destroying them."

Source: Etienne C. Wenger and William M. Snyder, *Harvard Business Review,* January–February 2000

conscious efforts to elevate communities from an informal way of working to a more formal way. In doing so, they have demonstrated that using communities creates an institutional KM approach, while allowing a large measure of localized (by geography, topic, or discipline) KM focus. The elements that must be in place to develop and evolve communities include:

- sponsorship,
- membership,
- roles and responsibilities,
- accountability and measurement, and
- supporting tools.

Like any new organizational form, CoPs need nurturing and support; this includes financial resources. The World Bank sees the flow of knowledge in communities as a primary driver in its KM activity. Therefore, it has allocated one-third of its KM budget directly to CoPs.

CoP Challenges

It is not particularly easy to build and maintain communities within an organization. Identified below are some of the most common challenges faced when integrating communities into the business:

- The CoP must reflect a necessary and natural grouping of people to create and share knowledge. Because these people often work and report in separate units, boundary spanning and sponsorship are essential.
- Supply-driven efforts are rarely successful. In the early stages of managing knowledge, companies often try, with little success, to build knowledge collections based on existing materials and without an active community of practitioners contributing to the effort. CoPs need to contribute and maintain their content, not have it created for them.

- It's difficult to make people collaborate; they must see as well as experience the value of interaction. Community formation requires significant face-to-face interaction. A critical success factor for Xerox was its hands-on approach to implementing Eureka. The Eureka team revisited those regions that showed low usage, and training was provided again through the use of examples. Reinforcing the purpose of the system helped encourage broad participation. Then the participation itself became rewarding.

- How does local community knowledge transcend the local context and personal experience of contributors to become critical knowledge for the global community? A process for screening and validating knowledge and best practices is essential. As a community convenes and discusses issues, the dialogue is captured so that it can be screened, filtered, and validated before it is provided as "organizational knowledge" to the enterprise.

The evaluation of community knowledge by selected or recognized experts in a particular field or focus area is a critical success factor for the validation process. These subject matter experts

ROADBLOCKS TO SUCCESS

- Being unclear about the desired results of the pilots
- Lack of skilled facilitators in the pilot groups
- Geographical dispersion of the pilot participants and lack of good IT collaborative tools to link them together

Expert Advice

- It is important that pilot efforts produce results, but it is equally important that the organization learn how to implement KM better. The stories of the pilots need to include the lessons learned as well as the business results.

- The facilitators and participants in these pilots and grassroots efforts will become the core team for future expansion. They need to form their own community and develop their own methods for sharing lessons and methods, as well as moral support.

(SMEs) lend credibility to the knowledge. The SMEs verify that individual knowledge should become community knowledge and indicate whether it could be used by other communities or teams in the organization. It also is important to note that organizations have learned that establishing a time frame for the validation process keeps knowledge entries from becoming stale and discouraging contribution.

Celebrating heroes, incorporating KM behaviors in performance expectations and appraisal, creating a validation process, and elevating knowledge experts and thought leaders to be leaders of CoPs are some of the ways organizations have addressed the KM challenges and change management issues associated with this new way of knowledge working.

CAPTURE LESSONS LEARNED

Perhaps the most important role of the KM practitioners and oversight group near the end of this stage is to capture lessons learned. What made the pilots most successful? Are the results worth investing for expansion? Are people or units clamoring to be involved and use the tools? Are other grassroots efforts popping up?

The oversight group should build a "lessons learned" discussion into its regular meetings. The agenda for this can be created by the facilitators. The oversight group and facilitators often form their own community and create a common space for sharing and saving lessons learned and stories of how problems were overcome.

After the pilots, the decision about the future of KM can go one of three ways:

1. expand and support the KM efforts, in which case a new strategy and budget are required;
2. improve the existing efforts, which usually leads to pushing the responsibility for maintenance of the pilots back to the business units; or
3. do nothing, which often means the employees collectively will revert to prior behavior as people who knew how to make KM work leave the unit.

<u>LANDMARK FOUR</u>

Expand and Support

By the time an organization reaches Stage 4, knowledge management has proved valuable enough to be officially expanded to become part of the organization's funded activities. Demand for KM support by other parts of the organization tends to be high, providing additional evidence of its value. Pilot results are an added benefit.

As advanced KM practitioners know, high visibility and the authority to expand are a mixed blessing. The added costs and visibility of resources devoted to KM will require more formal business evaluation and ROI justification. The good news is that unless unforeseen factors derail the efforts, KM is on its way to being considered a strategic and necessary competency.

KEY ACTIVITIES IN STAGE 4
1. Develop an expansion strategy.
2. Communicate and market the strategy.
3. Manage growth and control chaos.

DEVELOP AN EXPANSION STRATEGY

The first step is to develop an expansion strategy to ramp up KM throughout the organization. We have seen two approaches to expansion. The first is to apply the criteria for pilot selection to another round of units. The second option for expansion is to develop an all-at-once strategy.

Based on Stage 3, HP Consulting developed a four-step model for replicating the rollout of its KM initiatives in additional units:

1. Determine the KM business strategy and tactics.
2. Implement the technical and KM infrastructure.
3. Conduct orientation and deploy support teams.
4. Capture key lessons and revise the KM deployment plan.

The KM team focused on augmenting capabilities globally. In order to build skills, the team developed a philosophy to leverage available internal skills. When hiring from the outside, the team found candidates with knowledge-sharing capabilities and trained them on HPC's knowledge management processes. As HPC moved into this new phase, the team refined the existing KM roles and created new roles in the organization.

ShareNet was expanded throughout Siemens' Information and Communication Networks (ICN) Company by orchestrating a global rollout to 39 countries. The strategy included local top management buy-in and re-engineering of management processes, as well as training end users and ShareNet managers. The organization has achieved a return on investment ratio of 10:1.

There were many training and staff development activities associated with the global rollout for ICN ShareNet. ShareNet managers were trained during a "boot camp," the purpose of which was not only to train the ShareNet managers on the technical aspects of the knowledge management tool but also to build a high-value social network of ShareNet managers. Due to the simplicity of the knowledge base, only a half-day of technical training was required. Additional support is provided on an as-needed basis. The training is conducted by the local ShareNet managers and/or by members of the ShareNet Business Transformation Partner rollout team.

Another organization, The World Bank, decided to expand all at once. The organization's basic game plan was to articulate an explicit strategy, make a budget available for thematic groups (CoPs) and knowledge librarians, and provide suitable technology to allow the business units to proceed with implementation.

There are four important topics that arise during a global expansion: resources, language, culture, and information technology.

Resources

In every case, a leadership group and a core of facilitators and CoP leaders are needed. At Siemens, the Corporate KM group and the CoP KM, composed of more than 300 people in the business units, form the core resources. A chief knowledge officer (CKO) has been appointed, and the central KM group has developed a variety of templates, strategies, and tools for other groups to use to launch additional KM efforts.

Language

For firms that operate globally, addressing language and cultural issues is imperative. At Xerox, language barriers are overcome through the use of IT. Eureka, a knowledge-sharing system enabled by a portable database that technicians carry on their laptops out in the field, helps disseminate the knowledge. Technicians consult the database when trying to resolve issues with Xerox machines. They enter into the database a solution they have encountered in the field, and it is then validated before being posted for all technicians to see. Eureka operates in countries all over the world. In the new Eureka system, a tip is translated into English by the validator (using a translation software tool), posted to the system, and flagged with an icon of the original country in which the tip was created. A technician from that country can click on the flag, and the tip then becomes available to him/her in the language in which the tip was originally created.

Culture

All organizations can identify significant cultural and behavioral changes that must occur to create a knowledge-sharing organization. These changes often are referred to pessimistically as barriers when, in fact, any change is difficult. This journey is rarely without potholes.

In the early stages of knowledge management, HP Consulting found functional silos to be the most significant cultural barrier, even though more advanced firms do not (Figure 4). It is not that firms farther along in KM have not experienced silo mentality; rather it is that they, like HP Consulting, have identified means to overcome the obstacle.

We asked the best-practice partners in a recent APQC knowledge management consortium "What are the major drivers that help create a knowledge-sharing culture?"[2] It is clear that advanced firms are reaping the gains from the CEO's vision. The responses also confirm that human networks are key at any stage.

FIGURE 4: Cultural Issues in HP Consulting	
Cultural Barrier	**Addressing the Issue in HP**
Functional Silos	Solicit senior leadership vision and active support.
Headquarters vs. the Field	Involve users during design and implementation.
Language and Culture Differences	Accommodate learning and sharing styles as well as provide translation tools.
"Fuzzy Concept" or "Bells and Whistles" Computer System	Develop operational KM definitions tied to business needs.
Perception of KM as a "Bells and Whistles" Computer System	Concentrate on knowledge-sharing needs and behaviors; IT is an enabler.
Lack of Participation	Find and capitalize on passion, provide appropriate training, and use multiple channels for communication and promotion.

[2] *Successfully Implementing Knowledge Management, APQC, 2000.*

For advanced firms (n=10), the following were major drivers that created a knowledge-sharing culture:
1. CEO's vision included knowledge sharing.
2. Human networks created strong knowledge-sharing relationships.
3. Learning disciplines were reinforced through rewards, training, special events, and requirements.

For firms just starting out in knowledge management (n=24), the following were major drivers:
1. Knowledge sharing was tied to the business strategy.
2. Human networks created strong knowledge-sharing relationships.
3. Knowledge sharing was integrated with our daily work.

Information Technology Tools
Appropriate information technology is essential to KM expansion, especially for virtual teams communicating information to all units. In Chevron, the corporate IT group is now working with senior executives to reinforce knowledge sharing and reuse as fundamental corporate values and not simply as tools. Even though available technology makes it possible to design applications that will work worldwide, the issues of supporting users still have to be addressed. Chevron's corporate home page has been used as an advertising vehicle for initiatives such as the intranet knowledge map (find.Chevron), CBEST (Chevron's Business Electronic Support Tools), and the KM portal. Demonstrations of the tools have been provided for corporate groups, business teams, and an intranet council (a cross-operating company group that is helping to develop corporate standards, share useful Web applications, and promote the intranet as a primary communication and work tool).

COMMUNICATE AND MARKET THE STRATEGY

Once the strategy has been developed, organizations communicate their KM initiatives and expansion strategy in a variety of ways. HP Consulting and the World Bank have incorporated KM training in the orientation of new staff members. At Chevron, trained quality coordinators carried the projects into their organizations. Senior Chevron executives were given hands-on demonstrations of the knowledge-sharing best-practice database. A resource map listing all of the best-practice transfer teams was printed and widely distributed.

The World Bank KM group looked for opportunities to inform people about KM and its role in the Bank's mission. For instance, in February 1997, when all operations managers were being informed about changes under way in the organization, knowledge management was included as one of three modules. Additional forms of communication at the World Bank included:

- regular staff meetings,
- open houses that presented knowledge management to several hundred people,
- a Knowledge Fair that reached several thousand people in the organization,
- a presence on the Web,
- brochures and pamphlets on knowledge management, and
- the World Development Report on knowledge for development.

At Siemens, some of the KM promotional activities included sending a letter of endorsement from the CEO of the ICN company to all local employees, publishing a ShareNet article in the local company paper, and placing ShareNet articles on the intranet with a link to ShareNet. Other key activities included e-mail with direct link into ShareNet to demonstrate the capabilities of ShareNet as a communication platform, speeches and online demonstrations, brochures, posters, and videos.

Xerox has developed a two-hour awareness training session for all Xerox associates worldwide. This module addresses how knowledge sharing links to Xerox cultural dimensions, customer expectations, and what new behaviors are expected from the employees to demonstrate knowledge sharing. The message being delivered during training is employees must learn to adapt principles of knowledge sharing to their work lives. The expected outcome of the training is to teach employees to assess how information is shared within their community, use knowledge-sharing approaches to address issues in the community's work practices, and increase productivity within their business units.

This awareness session is to be rolled out to the communities of practice first and will eventually touch all Xerox employees. The awareness module will be deployed through face-to-face meetings and a Web-based application with audio conference that enables a virtual meeting place.

Another high-visibility strategy in Xerox was for senior managers to sponsor their own knowledge-sharing projects. These projects, called "lighthouse projects," are in various stages of deployment. They are lighthouses for Xerox because they demonstrate senior management commitment to making a change. Additionally, the company has recognized a role model manager in knowledge sharing.

The knowledge management team also approached the CEO and suggested that if Xerox was serious about knowledge sharing, it needed to be included as part of the criteria for the President's Award. The CEO agreed, and accomplishments for knowledge sharing (reusing) are now a part of the evaluation for the award.

MANAGE GROWTH AND CONTROL CHAOS

One of the consequences of success is the explosion of local KM initiatives that typically occurs at this stage. Because of all of the visible support given to knowledge management in the World Bank, more than 124 thematic groups (i.e., communities of practice) now exist. The result has been a fairly energized program of activities, with managers and the core staff members quite committed to the knowledge management activities that they themselves have launched. It also has led to less-than-perfect coherence and consistency between units.

The various patterns of implementation can lead to confusion for people less involved. In the World Bank, a considerable amount of fragmentation was identified at the time of the External Evaluation Panel in April 1999. At that time, only 37 percent of participants in focus groups agreed that the Bank's knowledge resources on the Web were easily accessible, compared with 70 percent of participants seeing the thematic groups as adding value. The most important cause of this problem is the fragmentation of substantial knowledge resources on the intranet, which hampers those resources being easily found by interested users. Resources are variously located in the intranet knowledge management systems, on the external Web, in network Web sites, in some regional Web sites, and in thematic group workspaces. A major effort is under way to implement a consistent Web policy.

Information technology standards boards can be a great help. At the World Bank, a technology group spends about 50 percent of its time on technology issues related to knowledge management. It also has responsibilities for information management and the internal and external Web.

At Xerox, the information technology group encourages communities to assess all the software available at the company and pick that which fits its needs. The IT group also provides assistance in selecting software if the community is not sure what it needs.

Expert Advice

- A central cross-functional KM group has to create an expansion strategy and identify required resources.

- Resources to successfully support widespread KM initiatives are not automatically available and have to be conscripted or developed from other units.

- Communicating the KM strategy and its rationale to the organization requires the same kind of vigorous marketing as any other large-scale initiative.

- Rapid expansion will inevitably entail some confusion and missteps, which can be alleviated somewhat by an active, central, cross-functional group.

Beyond imposing some order through technology, Siemens officially formed the CKM organization on October 1, 1999, with the responsibility to provide common methodologies and tools for implementation.

In order to move to Stage 5, Institutionalize Knowledge Management, several of the advanced KM organizations that APQC has examined conducted internal assessments of how their KM efforts were working. By looking at successes and gaps in the KM strategy, they developed recommendations and tools to close identified gaps:

1. At Chevron, the corporate KM group reviewed its efforts and made recommendations to management.
2. The World Bank engaged an outside team of KM practitioners to assess strengths and weaknesses in its strategy and deployment.

3. Xerox has embedded KM evaluation into its Xerox Management Model assessment process. This includes formally building KM-related items into the areas to address in the assessment (built on the Baldrige model) and asking questions about knowledge sharing in the monthly employee survey. These assessment efforts significantly shaped the planned improvement and strategy for moving forward to institutionalization.

Institutionalize Knowledge Management

In some ways, Stage 5 is the continuation of Stage 4 to its logical conclusion of full enterprisewide deployment. However, Stage 5 differs from Stage 4 in three fundamental ways:

1. It does not happen unless KM is embedded in the business model.
2. The organization structure must realign to reach Stage 5.
3. Evidence of knowledge management competency must become part of formal performance evaluation.

At Stage 5, sharing and using knowledge become part of the organization's "way of doing business" as well as an expected management competency.

In the relatively young arena of KM, only a few organizations have reached this stage. Of the advanced firms APQC has visited, the World Bank is in the early days of this phase. Xerox's Eureka approach in the Customer Service Organization is already well established as a way of working for field technicians in those many countries with access to the system. Xerox's corporate strategy probably is in Stage 4, but the strategic intent is to reach Stage 5. Siemens' ICN company has successfully deployed its KM approach worldwide. Within HP Consulting, KM is now part of the business model, and other changes are under way. Of the companies APQC has followed for many years, Buckman Laboratories is closest to aligning all of its management systems and processes around knowledge sharing, capture, and reuse.

Based on these experiences and our experiences institutionalizing other competencies such as process management, TQM, and team-based operations, APQC can make a good case for what is needed here.

KEY ACTIVITIES IN STAGE 5
1. Embed KM in the business model.
2. Realign the organization's structure and budget.
3. Monitor the health of KM.
4. Align rewards and performance evaluation.
5. Balance a common framework with local control.
6. Continue the journey.

EMBED KM IN THE BUSINESS MODEL
An organization does not reach Stage 5 unless KM is part of the business model; nor does it win CEO and senior executive support until it is in place. Best-practice organizations rely on the powerful support afforded by the CEO's vision, unlike the early stage adopters, which are still more reliant on networks of people to drive knowledge management (Figure 5).

In January 1999 the World Bank formally adopted poverty reduction as a goal. Further, the mission statement now includes

FIGURE 5: What Most Impacts the Creation of a Knowledge Culture?		
	Advanced Firms	Early Stage Adopters
CEO's vision includes knowledge sharing	70%	33%
Human networks create strong knowledge-sharing relationships	40%	58%

The World Bank's Mission Statement

To fight poverty with passion and professionalism for lasting results. To help people help themselves and their environment by providing resources, sharing knowledge, building capacity, and forging partnerships in the public and private sectors.

sharing knowledge as an enabler. This step has highlighted the impossibility of achieving the mission only through lending and hence underlined the crucial role that knowledge will have to play in the future.

At Xerox, several steps have been taken to embed knowledge management in the business model.

- Knowledge sharing was defined as one of the Xerox cultural dimensions and the way Xerox delivers value to the shareholders. By making it part of the cultural dimensions, sharing was put in business context.
- Knowledge sharing was added to the Xerox Management Model and integrated into the business assessment process. All senior managers are involved in the assessment process and given the resulting scores.
- Knowledge sharing was announced as a major initiative in the company's most recent reorganization.

The Xerox Management Model is the framework for how Xerox conducts business. It revolves around customer and market focus and includes internal elements for leadership, human resources, business process management, and knowledge and information. The foundation of this model is based on the Malcolm Baldrige National Quality Award criteria, which Xerox has adapted. In 1999 the category of "information utilization and quality tools" was revised to "knowledge and information." The elements under knowledge and information are knowledge sharing, quality and productivity tools, and information management.

Knowledge management has been ordained as a key management competency and competitive differentiation at Xerox. Although it is clear how knowledge management fits into Xerox's market position, the KM group is still struggling to find the resources to support it.

This illustrates one striking difference between early stage adopters and advanced firms. Advanced KM practitioners see financial support as one their biggest issues (Figure 6). Once KM becomes part of the mainstream and part of the normal budgeting process, it is subject to the same expectations and pressures of any other function. Early stage adopters should expect that the realities of organizational life will catch up with knowledge management; they can expect financial pressure to increase as they move through the stages.

On the other hand, advanced firms don't report that functional silos are a barrier, and early stage adopters see it as one of the biggest barriers they face. Early stage adopters ranked both lack of incentives and lack of definition as their primary obstacles to implementing KM in their organizations. CEO support probably breaks down functional barriers; advanced firms have it, and early stage adopters don't.

FIGURE 6: Top Obstacles to Successfully Implementing KM	
Advanced Firms	**Early Stage Adopters**
1. Internal politics	1. Lack of incentives
2. Financial support	1. Lack of definition and formalized strategy
3. Competitive pressures	2. Functional silos
4. Wrong perception of need	3. Financial support
5. Barriers to change	

REALIGN THE ORGANIZATION'S STRUCTURE AND BUDGET

In July 1999 the leadership of the KM group at the World Bank was shifted to Operations rather than the CIO's office. The shift signified that KM was a business strategy, not a database.

In 1997 the World Bank's budget for knowledge management was $13 million. That grew to $55 million in 1998, with only $36 million of that amount being spent. In 1999 the budget remained $55 million, and $57 million was spent. The budget for knowledge management has grown to $57 million for 2000; it represents 3 percent of the total Bank Group Operations (not lending) budget. Of that 3 percent, 91 percent is spent on operations to support KM and 9 percent is spent on IT.

This budget is not all "new money." It included consolidation of budgets from a variety of activities that had been contributing to the knowledge management effort and were now part of the formal organization and budgeting process for KM. Sector boards now control much of the budget for thematic groups.

At Xerox, deployment of knowledge management is now part of the Quality and Knowledge Sharing Organization, with oversight by its director. Skilled change agents and facilitators from the Xerox quality community are now part of the conjoint group.

Efforts to take KM to the "next generation" at Chevron were triggered by a partnership between IT and Corporate Quality to work with Chevron groups actively developing knowledge-sharing applications and practices. The KM council is an informal communication mechanism that shares good ideas. The intranet council, with representatives from major operating companies, meets regularly to share good practices and applications.

At Siemens, the business case for establishing the CKM office was the ability to leverage the large bodies of KM experience throughout Siemens into a joint KM strategy to develop a significant competitive advantage for the organization.

To move from expansion to institutionalization, Siemens CKM has two objectives:

1. extend expertise from beyond implementation tools to support tools for a sociotechnical knowledge management system; and
2. reduce the many similar knowledge management systems to a reasonable, small set of standardized approaches and speed up the implementation of additional systems.

CKM is now responsible for management and further development of cross-group best-practice sharing and develops it for all relevant cross-section topics in the company. There are two basic concepts: the best-practice sharing employee network (CoPs) and best-practice marketplace (mailing list, workshops, "project mall" and intranet site). Both concepts have already been developed and piloted.

Typically, the advanced knowledge management firms that APQC has studied formalize the KM support organization and appoint a person as overall coordinator, sometimes with the title of chief knowledge officer. Most continue to have business units responsible for implementation (decentralization). Centralized groups are provided and act as human and electronic contact for people who have questions and need information and support.

CKOs need to have two competencies: to understand how information technology can contribute to capturing, storing, exploring, and sharing knowledge; and to create social environments that facilitate willingness to spend time in knowledge capture and reuse (e.g., change agents.) They are able to develop events and processes to encourage deliberate knowledge creation and exchange. CKOs also are consultants, trafficking in ideas that fit the corporation's knowledge vision.

One of the CKO's jobs is to create high-level sponsorship beyond visible CEO support. Senior executives and prominent line managers must believe KM offers clear advantages to their mission.

MONITOR THE HEALTH OF KM

Several methods are in place to monitor the health of knowledge management in the best-practice organizations APQC has studied. As mentioned earlier, the World Bank convened a KM Evaluation Panel of external practitioners to conduct an in-depth assessment of KM. The practitioners made significant recommendations, which the Bank has adopted. The World Bank also conducts ongoing surveys to examine employees' understanding of KM, how they use it, and how useful it is for them.

Similarly, Siemens CKM conducts, upon request, a maturity evaluation of a business unit's KM activities.

Xerox sent a strong signal about its seriousness with regard to KM when it added knowledge sharing to its annual employee survey. For the first time, the employee survey will include four yes/no items addressing knowledge management:

1. Knowledge sharing is role-modeled by the organization's senior management.
2. I work in an environment where knowledge sharing characterizes the way we work.
3. In our organization employees are recognized/rewarded for sharing knowledge.
4. I understand the value of knowledge sharing as it relates to Xerox business strategy.

ALIGN REWARDS AND PERFORMANCE EVALUATION

Changing the performance appraisal system to include knowledge sharing is a far more dramatic move than simply providing awards and recognition to those who are role models in KM. Performance appraisal is the basis for promotion and pay and therefore is core to what the organization wants as competencies and behaviors in staff members.

In February 1999 the World Bank incorporated knowledge-sharing activities (including participation in thematic groups) into its performance evaluation forms.

In the current Hewlett-Packard Consulting evaluation model, everyone is evaluated on knowledge mastery. All employees must be able to understand the concept of a knowledge-based business model. Other factors included in performance evaluation are:

- commitment to ongoing learning, reusing, creating, and contributing to intellectual capital;
- written documentation of KM into the career structure affecting how people get promoted;
- support of a sharing culture with balance between innovation and reuse; and
- interaction with the network of resources to share and leverage global knowledge.

Other recognition awards are important as well. In 1999, HP Consulting created the Knowledge Masters Award. It is a prestigious annual award that recognizes and rewards employees whose knowledge mastery best exemplifies the culture of balancing innovation with reuse and contributes to significant and measurable business impact. Winners receive companywide recognition and an all-expense-paid trip or a cash award. In 1999, 182 nominees were submitted, resulting in 41 winners.

Siemens ICN users can receive ShareNet Shares. The number of shares an end user earns depends on the quality and reusability of the contribution—assessed through a peer rating. After the first year of ShareNet operation, the top contributors were invited to the ShareNet global knowledge-sharing conference and rewarded.

Xerox Worldwide Customer Services is sponsoring a Eureka Hall of Fame to recognize and reward Eureka users. Authors of solutions that resolve the greatest number of problems (or problems with large dollar savings) will be entered into the Hall of Fame and will receive cash awards and recognition (e.g., Eureka shirts with the Hall of Fame logo).

At Chevron, sharing knowledge and mentoring others are components of its technical career ladder, criteria for promotion, and job evaluation. The plan is to strengthen these elements and add specific metrics to measure what was shared and reused.

BALANCE A COMMON FRAMEWORK WITH LOCAL CONTROL

One of the challenges of making KM part of the business model is that divisions within the business will certainly actualize the model in their own autonomous way. At the World Bank, large-scale experimentation has been encouraged so that learning by doing can occur. A lack of consistency is a natural result. Significant efforts are now under way to enhance consistency and tighten linkages between business goals and knowledge management activities, particularly when using KM to enhance the quality of lending.

The knowledge management leaders at the World Bank believe this fragmentation reflects the needs of individual units and groups and makes the units appear distinctive—sometimes at the expense of the institutional need to present knowledge resources in a consistent and well-organized fashion to all users.

It is clear that KM has to "go native" for acceptance, but it is also clear that some common standards and policies can help. Business need should drive the formulation of the policy, and not the details of how a unit deploys it. Even the policy should be determined by practitioners, and the common institutional policy should allow variation where needed. The exception is for knowledge repositories that must be shared across the enterprise.

Hewlett-Packard's KM team enlisted a Standards Board from within the organization to set consistent guidelines and implement standards. The board establishes standards for the HP Consulting services portfolio and structured intellectual capital. The Standards Board consists of a cross-section of the organization and includes people who are of moderate to high levels in the organization (from finance, IT, business process and quality, field, solution development, and Consultants Knowledge Group). The people who were asked to be on the Standards Board were well respected and tended to have a broad view of HP Consulting's needs.

CONTINUE THE JOURNEY

In November 1997 knowledge management became part of business strategy for Hewlett-Packard Consulting. In 1998 a knowledge functional group was chartered, and in November 1999 KM was integrated into the global/regional business model. Currently there are more than 70 Learning Communities across the globe, and Project Snapshot competency has widened considerably. Consultant-driven demand for knowledge processes continues to rise, and the KM team in collaboration with the solution development areas have created Knowledge Maps for 25 percent of the organization's solutions.

According to HP Consulting, significant progress has been made toward transforming the organization into a true knowledge-sharing enterprise. The Knowledge Masters award continues to attract high interest in the consultant community, and the stories of time and money savings have been exemplary. Further, the KM team has developed a global knowledge repository and is actively managing its content. The appointment of knowledge managers for every key functional area is evidence of senior leadership support of this effort.

In looking forward, HP Consulting's critical success factors for continuing its journey toward institutionalizing KM are:

- leadership needs to be committed and involved;
- vision has to be inspiring, motivating, and consistent;
- steps to get to vision should be evolutionary, not a "big bang";
- a readiness assessment must be used to be able to start with change-ready groups (take the path of least resistance, and go where people are ready to start and work);
- role models—exemplars and successes that are tied to business results—must be identified; and
- communicate, communicate, communicate—use voice mail, newsletters, the Internet, e-mail, etc.

Currently, Siemens AG has more than 80 KM projects, with one-fourth of the projects having a considerable number of users, containing a large amount of content, and exhibiting an advanced state of implementation/operation. Two of the most mature projects are the ICN company and Corporate Procurement and Logistics.

The World Bank has included knowledge sharing in its mission statement, has more than 120 thematic groups, and has a $57 million budget for knowledge management.

As part of its continuing deployment of knowledge management as a business imperative, the World Bank has established increasingly tighter links between knowledge management and the business strategy. This has included moving the leadership of knowledge management out of the computer group and into an operations network, as well as establishing a workshop on the links between quality assurance and knowledge management. Knowledge sharing is now one of four core behaviors for all staff members and managers in the organization. KM is now part of the strategic planning process.

The next focus at Chevron will be on spreading the capture and reuse of knowledge through global communities of practice, best practices/lessons learned, continual improvement processes, and the Knowledge Connection and People Connection Web sites.

Based on APQC's study of knowledge management leaders, some predictions/assumptions can be made.

- E-Business will result in more ways to deliver more knowledge to customers and will extend to virtual collaboration with customers and business partners, creating new organizations and distributed work processes.
- Ways of building knowledge capture, sharing, and reuse into everyday work processes will continuously be pursued.
- Portals customized to deliver just-in-time information matching the preferences and roles of individual employees will become commonplace.

- Increasing bandwidth will make connections with international employees more practical, especially for sharing large, seismic data sets. Bandwidth also will lead to the proliferation of Web-based training, particularly streaming video. This may make video conferencing a more effective communication mechanism.
- For accounting reasons, measuring intellectual capital in a formal and consistent manner will become important.

KEY LEARNINGS

1. Stage 5 requires adoption of knowledge management as part of the organization strategy or mission. CEO and broad senior management support only comes if KM fits with the business model.
2. The organization structure will naturally change to better fit the new way of working.
3. KM is not really the "way we work" until it is part of the performance appraisal system.
4. Stage 5 is a journey, not a destination.

Packing List

Organizations at each stage of knowledge management implementation need resources to help them. The following are just a few essentials to aid your organization in its journey.

- APQC Membership
- Access to APQC's Best Practices Database™
- Consortium Learning Forums
- Focused Benchmarking Projects
- Publications
  - *If We Only Knew What We Know: The Transfer of Internal Knowledge and Best Practice*
  - *Knowledge Management: A Guide for Your Journey to Best-Practice Processes*
  - Best-Practice Reports
  - *inPractice* Case Study Series
  - Proceedings from APQC Knowledge Management Conferences

- APQC Knowledge Management Courses
  - KM 101: Managing Knowledge for Results
  - KM 201: Strategies for Leveraging Knowledge

- KM 301: Designing, Implementing, and Measuring KM Initiatives

- KM Consultative Offerings
  - Knowledge Audit
  - KM Strategy Development
  - Internal Benchmarking and Identification and Transfer of Best Practices
  - Pilot Strategy
  - Pilot Selection
  - Pilot Scope Statements and Charter
  - Business Case for Knowledge Management
  - Lessons Learned Capture
  - Expansion Strategy Creation
  - Customized Training

- Other Resources
  - Knowledge Management Assessment Tool (KMAT)
  - Knowledge Management Success Stories and Best Practices
  - Public and Custom Education Courses
  - KM Conferences

For more information about these products and services, contact APQC at 800-776-9676 (713-681-4020 outside the United States) or visit our Web site at www.apqc.org.

About the Authors

Carla O'Dell, Ph.D.

Dr. Carla O'Dell is president of the American Productivity & Quality Center and serves as director of its International Benchmarking Clearinghouse.

Dr. O'Dell's work in knowledge management dates back to 1995, when APQC and Arthur Andersen conducted the nation's largest symposium on KM with more than 500 attendees. Based on issues raised at the symposium, APQC launched, under Dr. O'Dell's direction, its first knowledge management consortium study, Emerging Best Practices in Knowledge Management, with 39 organizations. She also led APQC's second study, Using Information Technology to Support Knowledge Management, with 25 of the world's leading KM organizations.

Dr. O'Dell is co-author with Dr. C. Jackson Grayson of *American Business: A Two-Minute Warning,* which Tom Peters said "gets my vote as the best business book in 1988." Also with Dr. Grayson, Dr. O'Dell co-authored *If Only We Knew What We Know: The Transfer of Internal Knowledge and Best Practice,* published in 1998 by Simon & Schuster. She publishes several business journal articles each year.

A frequent keynote speaker at senior executive events who appears often on business television, Dr. O'Dell holds a bachelor's degree from Stanford University, a master's degree from the University of Oregon, and a Ph.D. in industrial and organization psychology from the University of Houston.

Farida Hasanali

A project manager with significant experience in knowledge management, Farida Hasanali has served in several roles at APQC over the past eight years. She has led and been involved in numerous consortium studies, including four that focused on knowledge management.

Hasanali, whose expertise includes information technology, practices internal knowledge management at APQC while serving in an IT role. She now focuses on methods of transferring learnings to APQC customers.

A presenter at several knowledge management events, Hasanali holds a bachelor's degree in psychology from St. Xavier College in Bombay, India.

Cindy Hubert

Cindy Hubert is a senior consultant in knowledge management at the American Productivity & Quality Center. Her focus is on business process improvement—knowledge management, transfer of best practices, quality, benchmarking, measurement, and strategic planning. Hubert is responsible for delivery of APQC's KM education and training courses, facilitation of knowledge management assessments, project management, transfer of best practices, course design, internal and external benchmarking studies, and instructor training.

Hubert has worked with a variety of industries including oil and gas, manufacturing, healthcare, financial, retail, nonprofit, and consumer products. Through her collaboration with Dr. Carla O'Dell, president of APQC, the Center has become a national leader in conducting and producing knowledge management studies, workshops, and publications. She has spoken frequently about knowledge management issues and practices and has conducted several workshops in the United States and abroad.

Hubert is a graduate of the University of Texas at Austin with a bachelor's degree in marketing and extensive experience in accounting and finance. She is a founding member and past president of the Sterling Group, a professional women's organization, and has served as an instructor of Knowledge Management & the Transfer of Best Practices at Rice University's Executive Education Graduate School of Management.

Kimberly Lopez

Kimberly Lopez is a custom solutions specialist with the American Productivity & Quality Center. Since joining APQC in 1998, she has been involved in numerous individual and consortium studies in the areas of higher education, human resources, and knowledge management. Lopez is trained in client facilitation, project management, and detailed survey analysis.

Prior to working at APQC, Lopez served in the intellectual property area. Her positions included intellectual property system consultant for a leading online information company and program coordinator for the University of Houston Law Center's intellectual property program. She has been a guest lecturer on various property-related topics.

Lopez holds a bachelor's degree in political science from the University of St. Thomas and an MBA from the University of Houston.

Peggy Odem

Peggy Odem recently served as an associate director at the American Productivity & Quality Center. With more than 20 years of experience focusing on performance improvement, benchmarking, measurement, and quality, she also has worked in the area of knowledge management, conducting consortium research studies, performing knowledge management assessments, and developing educational offerings for APQC.

Odem served as project manager for APQC's first three knowledge management consortium studies. She has been a presenter at several knowledge management conferences, both in North America and Europe, and has published and contributed to several articles. Odem has provided a wide range of services relating to key business issues such as performance measurement, strategic use of information and technology, leadership effectiveness, and, most importantly, alignment of these components toward a common set of results. She played a large role in APQC's Education Initiative by leading its benchmarking and performance improvement services.

Odem received her master's degree in health services administration from the University of Houston and bachelor's degree from Nicholls State University in Thibodaux, Louisiana.

Cynthia Raybourn

Cynthia Raybourn is an experienced consultant and trainer focusing on quality, benchmarking, measurement, and human resource initiatives. She has nearly 20 years' experience working with manufacturing, service, government, and academic organizations.

Raybourn has held several positions at the American Productivity & Quality Center, including director of education and training. She was a member of the team that planned and launched the International Benchmarking Clearinghouse, was involved in the creation of APQC's Best Practices Database™, and has been involved in numerous benchmarking studies. Raybourn also participated in APQC's first action research project in white collar productivity, the White House Conference on Productivity, and the development of the Texas Quality Award. In addition, she has written numerous articles for APQC publications.

Raybourn has a background in corporate communication and gained extensive experience in marketing and public relations prior to joining APQC. She received her bachelor's degree in speech communication from Pan American University and was a teaching fellow at the University of Houston while pursuing a master's degree in communication.

About APQC

F ounded in 1977, the Houston-based American Productivity &
Quality Center provides the knowledge, training, and methods
that empower businesses and other organizations to maximize their
potential with a focus on productivity, quality, and best practices.
APQC is a nonprofit organization and an internationally recognized
leader in benchmarking and best-practice information, serving its
500-plus members and other customers in all sectors of business,
industry, education, and government.

Over the years APQC has built a distinguished list of achieve-
ments, including providing private-sector input into the first White
House Conference on Productivity and spearheading the 1987
creation of the Malcolm Baldrige National Quality Award, which
we jointly administered for its first three years. In 1992 we created
the International Benchmarking Clearinghouse, a comprehensive
service co-designed with customers to facilitate benchmarking.
Our most recent venture is the APQC Education Initiative, a
special program designed to integrate business best practices into
educational institutions.

Today, APQC continues to work with organizations to improve
productivity and quality by providing the tools, information, and
support they need to discover and implement best practices and
obtain results in dozens of process areas.

For information on the many ways APQC can help meet your
organization's knowledge management and process improvement
needs, call 800-776-9676 (713-681-4020 outside the United States)
or visit our Web site at www.apqc.org. To see additional publications, go to www.store.apqc.org.